D0578018

FLOOR

furnishing

Cover-up in style –
25 stunning surface solutions

FLOOR
furnishing

Cover-up in style –
25 stunning surface solutions

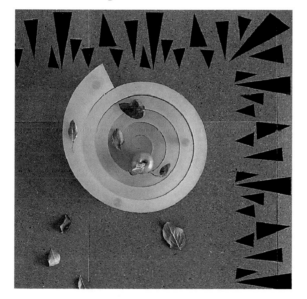

CATHERINE TULLY

PHOTOGRAPHY BY GRAHAM RAE

LORENZ BOOKS
NEW YORK · LONDON · SYDNEY · BATH

First published in 1996 by Lorenz Books

Lorenz Books is an imprint of
Anness Publishing Inc.
27 West 20th Street
New York, New York 10011

© 1996 Anness Publishing Limited

All rights reserved. No part of this publication may be reproduced, stored in a retrieval system,
or transmitted in any way or by any means, electronic, mechanical, photocopying, recording or
otherwise, without the prior written permission of the copyright holder.

ISBN 1 85967 234 5

Publisher: Joanna Lorenz
Photographer: Graham Rae
Designer: Caroline Reeves

PUBLISHER'S NOTE
The publishers have made every effort to ensure that all instructions are accurate and safe, and cannot
accept any liability for any resulting injury, damage or loss to persons or property however it may
arise. If in any doubt about the correct procedure to follow for any home improvement tasks, seek
professional advice.

10 9 8 7 6 5 4 3 2 1

Printed in Singapore

Printed in Singapore by Star Standard Industries Pte. Ltd.

CONTENTS

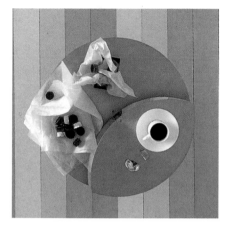

Introduction   6
Painted Floors   8
Rugs   10
Tiles   12
Decorative Baseboards   14
Embellished Baseboards   16

PROJECTS   18

Materials   84
Techniques   86
Templates   93
Index   96

INTRODUCTION

Floors are the very base of your living place and are often the first thing you

have to replace or renew when moving into a home. In previous years, people

wanted floors to last a lifetime. The major consideration was durability, and home-

owners spent as much as they could afford on their floors. Now we are much

more mobile and our homes are often seen as short- or medium-term

accommodations, because of work or the planned growth of the family.

We also change our furnishings more often, so today's ideal is chic and inexpensive

flooring that has instant design impact.

Contemporary flooring can be daring and fun and can incorporate lighter and less

expensive materials. If in doubt about a room's final use or color scheme, a beautiful,

neutral floor will allow you to be flexible. The scale of a room is also important: large

patterns are seen to best advantage only in large rooms with a minimum of furniture.

However, floors are often the main feature of halls and passages, even more so when seen

from an upper landing. In these venues, go for a really eye-catching floor treatment.

Practicality is also important. Consider whether the area is going to be exposed to water,

as in a bathroom, or to heavy wear, as in a kitchen, and whether durability is

paramount or a more whimsical surface is an option. But above all, choose projects that

appeal to you and that will give you floors you will

enjoy creating and for years to come.

PAINTED FLOORS

Above: Use different shades of wood stain for a restful effect. Here, the border of oak leaves was reverse-stenciled, then the details of the leaves were applied freehand.

If you are lucky enough to inherit a house that has naturally beautiful wooden floors, you may wish to do no more than add a decorative border. If the floor has been waxed or varnished it will be necessary to remove this layer first with a wood stripper or sander. Modern paints allow for a multitude of effects, but don't overlook wood stains, which can be used in combinations to produce subtle effects that are eminently suitable for a classic country home.

Stenciling has a folksy image that people associate with country style, but in reality, it is one of the most versatile floor treatments and one of the simplest. Either buy one of the many stenciling kits available or, if you are feeling more adventurous, photocopy a favorite motif, stick the photocopy to a sheet of acetate and cut out the stencil. Bold, geometric motifs are the easiest for novices both to cut and paint. If you are more experienced, you might like to try designs derived from flower shapes or more elaborate patterns.

When using color, remember a few basic principles: neutral tones always work well together but can be boring; complementary colors (red and green, yellow and purple) are very dramatic but can be overbearing; different tones of the same color, possibly with sharp accents in a much lighter or darker tone, are restful. Black and white are always good together and are a classic combination for halls, kitchens and bathrooms. Some of the paint effects in this book may look complicated, but if you follow the instructions carefully you will soon realize how very easy they are. Always remember that no paint effect need be permanent. If you tire of the design, strip the floor down and start again. Similarly, any signs of wear and tear that begin to show can be touched up. Varnishing is important. Once you have decided whether you want a matte or gloss finish, apply several coats of varnish to build up a really hard-wearing layer (make sure the room is well-ventilated). Some varnishes are available that have been specially formulated for floors, and though these are more expensive than conventional varnishes, generally only two or three coats are needed.

8

Above: Stamps are an easy way to decorate, and the variety now available ready-made is enormous. Use them for a simple but decorative edging, to give a hand-made quality that is totally in keeping with the natural wood floor.

Left: If you don't want, or can't afford, a patterned carpet, and your wooden floor is in good condition, create a unique and individual look, with just as much color and interest as a carpet, with stenciling. You can be as bold or as subtle as you like.

RUGS

If you don't want to embark on a complete change of flooring or if you're still making up your mind about changing the floor, they can disguise faults, add new color and textural interest, provide warmth and softness for your feet and help to soften the acoustics of a room with a lot of hard surfaces. Rugs are available in as many sizes, shapes, textures, colors and styles as home-owners can imagine. Some of the most precious silk rugs and carpets from Persia, Turkey and the Orient are extremely valuable, but equal ethnic style can be found at inexpensive street-markets. Classic and traditional styles are available to suit period interiors of every age and taste, but superb modern designs, which make focal points in the same way as a striking abstract painting hung over a mantelpiece, are equally easy to find. Making your own rugs opens up a limitless range of style options, provided you are not afraid to be bold.

Above: The classic interpretation: a perfectly simple, textured wool rug on a beautiful wooden floor. The simplicity and purity of the rug set off the subtle variations of color found in the floorboards.

Right: This isn't a traditional rug, but it would be at home in either a country-cottage-style or modern interior. The calm color scheme and the invocation of heavenly tranquillity make this rug especially suitable for a bedroom or study. It's unmistakably hand-made but far from lacking in sophistication.

Above: This is a classic folk-art-style rug.

Above: Unmistakably rustic, this rug would make an instant focal point.

Left: Made with a traditional hooking technique, this bath mat uses seashore colors to create a modern interpretation of the kind of homemade rug that was once found in bathrooms everywhere.

TILES

Above: Flagstones and tiles have long been popular, not just in cottages and farmhouses but in larger country houses too. These are laid in a traditional Victorian style, but if your home is not of that period, you could make a simple, modern pattern to equally dramatic effect.

Tiles are one of the most expensive forms of flooring, but they look beautiful and are very durable. Because of all these factors, be prepared to spend quite a lot of time before you actually lay the floor evaluating the many different tiles that are available. Don't be afraid to spend money if you find tiles you could really die for. Choose a cheaper alternative, and you may live to regret it. The terra-cotta tiles that are imported from countries in the Mediterranean and South America look gorgeous with their sunburnt colors. Hunting around architectural salvage yards can often yield an entire Victorian floor, but if you have no luck, most hardware or home decorating stores sell a wide range of alternatives. If you have the patience, a mosaic floor can look stunning, particularly where there is an open space and not much furniture, such as in a hallway, for example.

Right: Originally imported and copied from countries with a history of terra-cotta tiles, these are now available in such a vast variety that you can create a very individual floor just by choosing different finishes and sizes.

Above: A bathroom and kitchen standard for most of this century, ceramic tiles don't have to be boring. This interesting design is an eye-catching focal point in its own right, for an otherwise empty area such as a corridor. Combining elements of Islamic style, and with more than a hint of the mosaics that graced Roman buildings, this is a modern and engaging interpretation, perfectly illustrating the sheer versatility of tiles as a decorative medium for floors.

Above: Elegant marble is available quite cheaply now, particularly in this single gray color: most hardware or home decorating stores stock it. Though slightly daunting to cut and lay, marble tiles are the perfect cool, elegant solution in areas that are likely to be damp, such as bathrooms.

Above: Wooden flooring materials tend to make use of the same principles as tiles for their aesthetic effect: the combination of interlocking shapes and natural textures is enhanced here by the addition of the cool, clean metal of the heating grilles – a lesson in combining form and function.

DECORATIVE BASEBOARDS

Above: This is a striking baseboard, which would brighten up most rooms and would be an appropriate companion to, say, a striped floor or a plain floor which boasted a brightly patterned rug.

At the most mundane level, baseboards neaten up the area between the floor and the walls, and have the practical function of covering up any pipes and keeping out the cold air. They should not be neglected, as they supply the necessary visual tie between the two surfaces of the wall and floor.

In the past, most people were content to do no more than give their baseboards an occasional coating of gloss paint, but these days we are more creative. In a room decorated in soothing neutrals that is to be furnished perhaps with just a few very beautiful pieces of antique furniture, for instance, mimic the patina of the wood by coating the baseboards with matching woodstain. This can then be varnished to a gloss, matte or satin finish, whichever you think is most appropriate. If you don't mind the extra work, try sanding the last coat of varnish, then polishing with the same wax that you usually use on the furniture.

In another situation, you might prefer to be as bold and imaginative with your baseboards as you are with walls and floors. It would be dramatic to brighten an otherwise soberly decorated room with a lively patterned baseboard – like wearing a jazzy tie with a dark business suit. Or stick to the color scheme you have already chosen, perhaps by using a few of the colors in a more restricted space. A montage effect can also be fun, particularly if you can pick up a motif from the curtains, a cushion or some other item in the room. Cut out suitable pictures from a magazine or catalogue, or photocopy a favorite image several times. You can leave the images black-and-white or color them in with inks using an artist's brush. Stick them to the baseboard carefully with wallpaper paste, wipe off the excess and then varnish several times.

Top right: This is a very whimsical way to give your room an instant air of fun. The subjects for montages are endless; the only limitation is how good you are at cutting out intricate motifs. Since baseboards are not subject to wear, you can tell entire stories on yours; try a poem or a picture-and-word series running around the baseboard in an entryway.

Middle right: Add a note of color by painting the baseboard in a contrasting color, such as this distressed green, which still harmonizes perfectly with natural wood tones and textures.

Bottom right: For a natural wood floor, choose a complementary tone for the wood stain for the baseboard. Combined with neutral-colored walls, this is the classic treatment for modern and period-style interiors where the furnishings are the star of the show.

EMBELLISHED BASEBOARDS

Above: This looks like something left over from a medieval doorway or at least from the Wild West. Add really strong texture with metal studs; you could even apply pieces of leather and make a heavy-metal and biker-influenced baseboard.

If the surface of a baseboard strikes you as too flat and dull, give it a bit of texture by adding one of the embellishments suggested here. Hardware and home decorating stores are full of decorative beading and moldings that are intended for use on fiberboard furniture but which can be easily applied to baseboards (using the adhesive recommended by the manufacturer). It is easier to paint these and allow them to dry before applying, rather than painting them *in situ*. But don't let your imagination stop there. Experiment, for instance, with rope patterns on a flat surface. When you hit on one you like, draw the shape in pencil on the baseboard, then follow the outline with a line of glue. Allow this to become tacky, then press the rope into place. Either leave the rope in its natural color, dye it or spray it with metallic paint, for a real touch of Versailles splendor.

Some of the floor treatments in this book can be adapted easily to baseboards. The studded floor idea, for instance, is equally stunning when applied to the vertical surface. Or try cutting self-adhesive sheets of rubber mats into geometric shapes for a postmodern look. Whatever you do, make sure your baseboards are really "off the wall."

Right: Here, self-stick rubber mats were cut into wacky, postmodern embellishments; alternatively, play tic-tac-toe or just make the most of the texture, painting the rubber all one color.

Top right: Rope gives wonderful three-dimensional effects to your baseboards. Again, because the area doesn't suffer much wear and tear, it could be left au naturel for a back-to-nature look or painted gold or all white for a touch of operatic diva style.

Middle right: If you like a quirky, witty element in a décor scheme, this idea, which will certainly bamboozle visitors at first glance, is for you. Wooden moldings come in such variety that this rope molding, coupled with painted holes, is just one of many trompe l'oeil *effects you can achieve.*

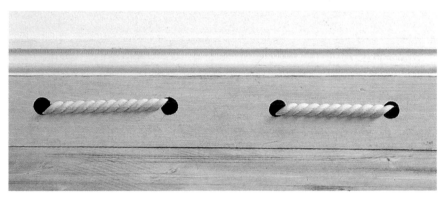

Bottom right: An elaborate paint effect here: a lightly marbled baseboard is embellished with gold-painted beading for a classy but divinely decadent look.

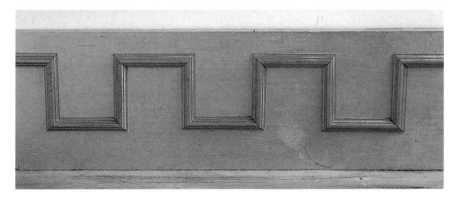

BUTTERFLY MONTAGE

Surrealism and the work of Ernst, Escher, Fornasetti and Magritte inspire the use of unusual yet familiar objects in designs for montages. This butterfly floor could just as easily have been made using motifs of flowers, boats or chairs. Strong lines are important, and books of wonderful line drawings are available. Lay the motifs down in an ordered pattern, rather than randomly. Here the design suggests the flight pattern of butterflies.

YOU WILL NEED

- light-colored emulsion paint
- paint roller
- motifs
- craft knife
- cutting mat
- wallpaper paste
- paintbrushes
- indelible felt-tipped pen or fine artist's brush and oil-based paints
- matte varnish

1 Make sure your floor is completely smooth. If necessary, lay a hardboard or marine-grade plywood floor (*see Techniques*). Paint the floor a light color so that the motifs will show up. Photocopy your chosen image(s) in at least seven sizes from small to large.

2 Using a craft knife, carefully cut out every image.

3 Decide on the positions of your images and stick them in place with wallpaper paste.

4 Add remaining fine details with a fine artist's brush and/or an indelible felt-tipped pen. Finish by applying at least six coats of varnish to be sure of its durability (some acrylic varnishes dry very quickly) or apply an especially strong floor varnish.

PASTEL STRIPES

Stripes are having a revival; they can transform a room, adding a light playfulness on a minimal budget. For maximum effect, keep your furnishings light and funky and add bright patches of unexpected color with small objects such as vases, chairs, flowers and so on. The alternating colors also allow you to bring in different cushions and curtains for different seasons. For a child's room, substitute bold reds, blues, yellows and greens for these pastel colors.

YOU WILL NEED
- ◆ masking tape
- ◆ pencil (optional)
- ◆ eggshell matte paint: lemon, pastel blue, pink and green
- ◆ paintbrushes
- ◆ matte varnish

1 Prepare your floorboards by securing any loose boards and sanding them (*see Techniques*). Bear in mind that the paint emphasizes any faults in the wood, so repair and sand the floor thoroughly. Test your color combination on a separate board.

2 Tape along the edges of every alternate board. You may find it helpful to indicate your color choice on each board in pencil, so you don't lose track of the order.

3 Starting with the lightest color, paint all the boards in between the ones edged with the masking tape. Leave the paint to dry then remove the tape and replace it on the painted boards. Paint all the boards in this way.

4 Finally, when the stripes are completely dry, apply two or three coats of varnish to seal.

PISTACHIO-SHELL BORDER

In India and the Far East, decoration on floors and walls is as varied as the materials available. The floors of temples and shrines are often intricately patterned with everyday natural objects. Taking this as inspiration, use seeds, shells, stones, bits of china, mirror fragments or anything else you can think of, as long as it has a flat surface. In these hot countries, soft sandals or bare feet are the norm; in this country, restrict your flooring with shells to the rooms in which you don't normally wear shoes. You can fill in just a small area or, if you just love pistachios, fill in your whole border. A simple corner measuring about 4 x 4 ft takes about 7 pounds of unshelled pistachio nuts.

YOU WILL NEED

- ◆ cream latex paint
- ◆ paint roller
- ◆ paint-mixing tray
- ◆ ruler
- ◆ pencil
- ◆ masking tape
- ◆ blue acrylic eggshell paint
- ◆ paintbrushes
- ◆ white glue
- ◆ pistachio shells
- ◆ natural sponge
- ◆ eggshell latex paint: peach, cream and pale blue

2 Measure and draw out your straight borders and edge them with masking tape. Draw your curved shapes straight onto the floor freehand or using a traced shape.

1 Make sure your floor surface is sound, dry and level; cover with hardboard or marine-grade plywood (*see Techniques*), if necessary. Apply a base coat of cream latex paint.

3 Fill in the lines with blue paint.

4 Apply a generous amount of white glue to the blue areas, working on a small area at a time. The glue should be quite thick. Apply pistachio shells to the glue, working on the fine areas first. You may find you need to sort the shells by size in advance.

6 To paint the area inside the border, start by sponging on the darkest color (in the photograph, peach) randomly; cover the whole area all at once.

8 Allow to dry and then use the same technique to apply a new color (in the photograph, pale blue) over it.

5 Once the glue is completely clear and dry, apply blue paint over the shells and touch up any areas of cream paint that need it.

7 Allow to dry completely and then repeat, using a softer shade of the same color (in the photograph, peach mixed with cream).

9 Seal the floor with watered–down glue as recommended by the manufacturer; it should be quite thick over the shells. The whiteness will disappear as it dries, leaving a clear surface. Allow to dry completely.

BOARD GAME CARPET TILES

Along with linoleum tiles, carpet tiles are real winners in the practicality stakes. Almost unbeatable in areas that need to be durable and where children spend a lot of time, carpet tiles have the single disadvantage that they never look like wall-to-wall carpeting, no matter how well they are laid. Rather than fighting the fact that they come in non-fraying squares, make use of this very quality and create a fun pattern, such as this giant board game. Carpet tiles are very forgiving, allowing for slight discrepancies in cutting, and are very easy to replace if an area is damaged. A geometrical design is easiest; it is advisable to leave curves to the experts, but anything else, from a board game to the elegance of a painting by Mondrian, is accessible.

YOU WILL NEED

- ◆ metal tape measure
- ◆ pencil
- ◆ paper
- ◆ carpet tiles
- ◆ white crayon or white pencil
- ◆ metal ruler
- ◆ craft knife and plenty of spare blades
- ◆ heavy-duty, double-sided carpet tape

1 Measure your room and make sure that the floor is level and all protruding nails have been flattened. Any flat surface will accommodate the carpet tiles, whether it is marine-grade plywood, hardboard, floorboards or concrete.

2 Plan your design on paper. Most rooms are not perfectly square or rectangular, so leave room for an area of plain tiles to edge the pattern.

3 Measure the tiles to determine the size of your pointed shapes and to work out how many tiles will be needed for your pattern. Consider the different weaves and nap of the carpet tiles and make them work to enhance your chosen plan. Using a white crayon or pencil, draw the pattern on the reverse of your tiles.

4 With the metal ruler and a craft knife, score along the marked lines. Don't attempt to cut the tile through completely in one stroke.

5 Starting at the top of the tile, cut down your scored lines. Do this on a solid surface and be extremely careful.

6 Lay down a line of carpet tape and remove the backing. Cut the tiles for a complete strip and fit these first, rather than laying little bits at a time.

7 Stick your cut tiles in place, making sure not to pack them too tightly. Begin by making the whole of the checkered border. Then fill in, laying strips of carpet tape as you work. Press the tiles down; uneven cuts will be unnoticeable.

Right: A chessboard would also make a good pattern for a floor.

STUDDED FLOOR

Create the look of the deck of a battleship, with studs at regular intervals painted in battleship gray, or leave the wood natural and the studs unpainted for a medieval banquet hall effect. The studs are called domes of silence because they are designed to be used under chair legs to help chairs glide across the floor without noise. However, you could use any studs, as long as they aren't sharp or liable to cause damage to shoes or furniture.

YOU WILL NEED

◆ pencil
◆ steel ruler or straightedge
◆ studs or "domes of silence"
◆ eraser
◆ acrylic varnish (optional)
◆ paintbrush (optional)
◆ tack hammer
◆ cloth or carpet scrap
◆ wood glue (optional)

1 Decide on the spacing and pattern of the studs or domes. Draw diagonal grid lines according to your design and mark where each stud is to go with a little cross. Erase all markings except the crosses.

2 If necessary, apply a couple of coats of acrylic varnish to the whole floor, to seal the wood.

3 Using a hammer and a buffer of something soft – such as a scrap of cloth or softwood – to prevent damage to the studs, hammer them in over the crosses. If you use domes of silence, which have relatively shallow teeth, hammer them in only part way to start with. Remove the domes, apply a little wood glue, then replace them and hammer them in all the way. This technique can be used on any decorative wooden floor.

STAMPS AND DRY BRUSH

Sometimes, when a room has unusual furnishings, it is good to give it a distinctive style by making a statement on the walls or floor. Here, the busy look of dry brush strokes combines with the simplicity of Japanese characters. The result is a warm yet stylish look that makes a memorable room.

YOU WILL NEED
- ◆ calligraphy brush
- ◆ black ink
- ◆ paper
- ◆ scissors
- ◆ paper glue
- ◆ foam block
- ◆ craft knife
- ◆ cream, rust-colored and white latex paint
- ◆ large and small paint roller
- ◆ dry paintbrush
- ◆ masking tape
- ◆ black and rust-colored paint
- ◆ matte varnish

1 Paint your Japanese characters with the calligraphy brush first, following the examples shown in this project. Make photocopies of each design.

2 Cut the characters out and glue one of each character to the foam. Keeping the knife at an angle, cut away all the white paper and the foam underneath to make a raised stamp.

3 Prepare the floor, hammering in any protruding nails, and make sure it is clean and dry. Give the whole floor a base coat of cream latex paint and allow to dry.

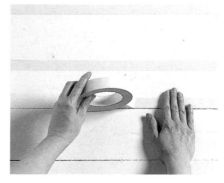

4 Using masking tape, tape off both edges of alternate boards ⟶

5 Draw a dry brush, dipped into a little rust paint, across the unmasked boards in a series of parallel strokes, allowing the base coat to show through in places.

6 Repeat this exercise with white paint, which softens the whole effect. Allow to dry, then repeat the procedure with both colors on the remaining boards.

7 Plan your design of Japanese characters, using spare photocopies of the characters, roughly cut out.

8 Using a small roller, ink some of the stamps with black ink.

9 Replace some of the photocopies with black stamped characters.

10 Repeat, using the rust-colored ink. Seal well with matte varnish and allow to dry.

PHOTOCOPY MONTAGE

This effect is reminiscent of the wonderful painted floors of European palaces. Few of us can afford to commission frescoes and floor painting, but you might still aspire to a home decorated fit for Marie Antoinette. Using photocopied images can make these dreams a reality. Choose any theme: the photograph shows a composition of landscapes, but architectural drawings, classical motifs, such as columns, garden urns and statues or even still-lifes of fruit, vegetables and china, could be made into successful montages. Using the same techniques, create a totally modern feeling using color photocopies of, say, flower heads; instead of stenciling the borders, add freehand leaves and scrolls.

YOU WILL NEED
- cream and green eggshell latex paint
- paintbrushes
- photocopied images
- long metal ruler
- craft knife
- cutting mat
- artist's watercolor or acrylic paints
- rubber cement tape (if necessary)
- pencil
- masking tape
- sheet of acetate
- tracing paper
- green stencil paint
- stencil brush
- wallpaper paste
- matte varnish

1 Starting with a well-prepared hardboard or marine-grade plywood floor (*see Techniques*), paint on an undercoat of cream eggshell paint, followed by a top coat. Allow to dry completely.

2 Experiment with images at different sizes and settle on an arrangement that looks good on your floor. Trim the images so that you are left with just the picture.

33

3 If your images are black-and-white, use watercolor or acrylic paints to put soft washes of color over the prints. You may need to stretch the paper, using rubber cement tape, depending on the quality of the paper (test a small area first).

4 Arrange the photocopies on the floor and plan and draw out the borders. Tape off the boxes where the copies will go with masking tape.

5 Paint between the lines of masking tape with green eggshell paint. When the paint is almost dry, gently peel off the masking tape to reveal crisply defined borders beneath.

6 For the stenciled borders, photo-copy the template at the back of the book to the required size, then place it over the acetate and cut it out with a craft knife on the cutting mat. For the smaller pattern areas, tape over unnecessary elements of your stencil using tracing paper and masking tape.

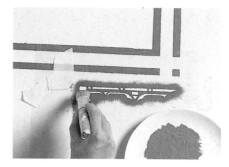

7 Apply the stencil to the floor with masking tape and stipple the stenciled border areas with green paint.

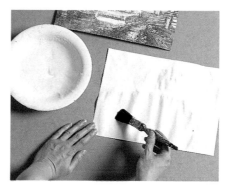

8 Spread the photocopies on the back with wallpaper paste, and position them on the floor. Varnish the floor several times.

Opposite: Create a floor with the feel of an eighteenth-century European palace by combining a montage of photocopied images with decorative stenciling.

DECKING OR DUCKBOARDS

The Japanese bathhouse is the inspiration for this floor treatment, which prevents pools of water from turning your bathroom into a skating rink and, at the same time, imparts the serenity of a Zen garden. In this project, the duckboards form a pontoon or walkway across the bathroom, but you could also use sections and cut them around the bathroom fittings. Ready-made decking is also available in strips or squares.

YOU WILL NEED

- tape measure
- saw
- base shoe
- duckboards or decking
- drill with wood bit and pilot bit
- wood stain
- soft cloth
- paintbrush
- wood screws

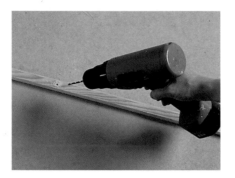

1 Make sure you have a clean, level floor: cork tiles, wood and linoleum are all suitable. The floor will show through, so if you want to change the color, do so now! Measure and cut the base shoe to the same length as the runners on the decking. Drill holes through these new runners.

2 Stain the two new long runners the same color as the duckboards.

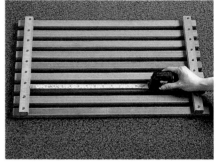

3 Measure the distance between the runners on the duckboard.

4 Space the new runners at a distance that will allow the duckboard runners to slide between them, holding the duckboard steady but allowing it to be lifted up for cleaning. Screw in place by drilling through the subfloor, using the correct type of bit for the type of floor you have. Slide the duckboards or decking into place.

PARQUET

Good parquet is a very manageable kind of flooring. There are numerous patterns to be made from combining these wooden blocks. A good trick is to work out the pattern starting from the center and make it as big a perfect square as you can; then lay a simple border to accommodate all the tricky outside edges. Parquet is often in oak, but you could dye it with stain or varnish for a richer effect.

YOU WILL NEED
- ◆ pencil
- ◆ ridged spreader
- ◆ floor adhesive
- ◆ parquet blocks
- ◆ wooden rod
- ◆ matte varnish
- ◆ paintbrush
- ◆ fine-grade sandpaper

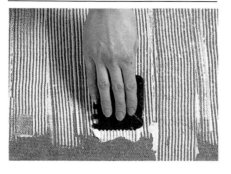

1 Make sure your floor surface is clean, dry and level. Find your starting point as for laying floor tiles (*see Techniques*) and draw guidelines on the floor. Using a ridged spreader, coat a manageable area of floor in floor adhesive.

2 Apply wood blocks to the adhesive. Use a wooden rod laid across the blocks to check that they all lie flush. Repeat until the floor is covered. Seal the floor with two or three coats of varnish, sanding between coats.

Above: You can make up lots of different patterns. The example here would be easy to do.

Above: Classic herringbone presents problems at the edges if the room is not perfectly square but could be combined with a simpler pattern around the outside.

FLOATING WOODEN FLOORING

Wood-strip flooring is one of the best ways to create instant elegance. It comes in a huge variety of finishes and lengths, so you can combine different woods without any major laying and fitting difficulties. Once you have grasped the principles of how to lay wood-strip, you can work out many different ways of laying it. The main photograph shows walnut interspersed with wide, light-colored maple boards. Alternatively, choose just one wood and lay it in different patterns. Wood-strip flooring is available in various types; the ones used here have ingenious metal clips that hold adjacent strips together. A wide range of wood varieties is available. Laminated types are generally pre-finished, but others need to be sealed once they have been laid.

YOU WILL NEED

- ◆ cushioned underlay (if necessary)
- ◆ tape
- ◆ metal joint clips
- ◆ hammer
- ◆ wood-strip flooring
- ◆ spacers
- ◆ wood glue
- ◆ saw
- ◆ tacks and quadrant beading (optional)
- ◆ pencil
- ◆ drill with wood bit

2 Prepare all the boards of wood-strip by hammering the special metal joint clips into the groove on the underside of the board, along the tongued edge.

1 Make sure that the subfloor is clean, dry and level. Then unroll the special cushioned underlay, if using, across the floor, taping one end to keep it in place.

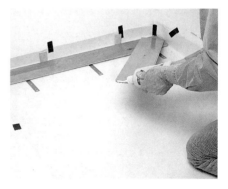

3 Lay the first length, clips toward you, against the walls, using spacers to create an expansion gap next to the wall. Glue the ends of the butt-jointed lengths.

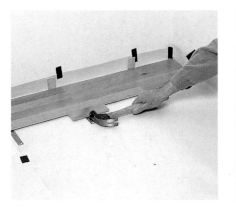

4 Position the second row of boards, tapping them together with a hammer and an offcut, so that the clips on the first row engage in the groove of the second.

6 Insert some protective packing against the wall before levering the strip into place. Make it level with a hammer, and protect the floor with a board offcut.

8 To fit a board around a pipe, mark its position and drill a suitably sized hole. Then cut out a tapered wedge, which can be glued back after fitting the board.

5 The last board is fitted without clips. Cut it to width, allowing for the spacers, as in step 3, and apply adhesive along its grooved edge.

7 Replace the baseboards, or fix a base shoe to hide the expansion gap; make sure the skirting fits tightly against the floor.

Above: If you want to vary the pattern of the flooring in the center of the room, as in the main photograph, lay your central boards at right angles to the boards around the outside, if the tongue-and-grooving permits. Three walnut boards followed by a maple board are used here.

COLOR-WASHED PARQUET

Herringbone patterns on floors give instant classical elegance, suggestive of the wonderful dark oak parquet floors found in the halls and ballrooms of large old houses. However, a younger, freer look is often wanted, with all the interest of the old floors; the introduction of a pale, soft color lifts gloomy dark wood into the realms of light Atlantic beach houses or modern Swedish homes. To keep the interest of the grain of the wood running in different directions, paint each individual piece separately; this can be further enhanced by subtle changes of color. If you are lucky enough to have a herringbone floor already, and have a certain amount of patience, masking the blocks individually before painting will give a more professional finish.

YOU WILL NEED
◆ marine-plywood, cut into manageable lengths
◆ miter saw
◆ tape measure
◆ sandpaper
◆ cream matte latex paint
◆ paintbrushes
◆ blue and white matte latex paint
◆ matte water-based glaze
◆ lint-free cloth
◆ floor adhesive
◆ matte varnish

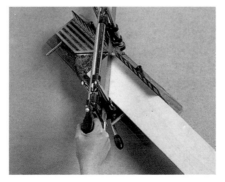

1 Make sure the floor is clean, dry and level. Miter the edges of the marine-ply strips, using a miter saw. Remember that you must have left- and right-hand miters in equal numbers.

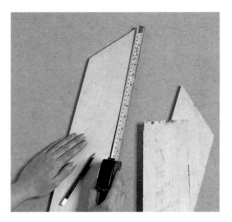

2 Measure your required length for the herringbone pattern and cut as many as you need for the floor.

3 Smooth any rough edges with sandpaper.

4 Undercoat all the boards with a warm cream paint and allow them to dry completely.

5 Mix up at least four variations of your main color with very little tonal difference between them. Add a little matte water-based glaze to each, to delay the drying time. Thin one of the colors with water to make it even more translucent.

6 Paint equal numbers of the boards in each color.

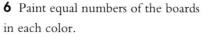

7 With the cloth, wipe off most of the paint randomly while it is still wet, so that the undercoat shows through. Wipe in the direction of the grain of the wood.

8 For an even more weathered look, sand some areas of some boards; this will give contrast when the floor is down. Lay the floor following the instructions for the Parquet project. Seal the whole floor with two coats of varnish.

Opposite: Give a wholly contemporary interpretation to traditional parquet flooring by color-washing the blocks individually. There is scope here for matching the floor to your decorative scheme in a more subtle and imaginative way than with a more straightforward painted floor.

POP-ART STYLE FLOOR

Much inspiration is to be gleaned from the pop artists of this century, with their whimsical approach to art. These naïve shapes painted on a large surface make use of the pop-art conventions of boldness and simplicity, with multiple repetitions of strong images rather than intricate designs. Slightly discordant colors – orange and shocking pink in this case – are the most appropriate. This idea is best for a concrete floor.

YOU WILL NEED
- ◆ white matte latex paint
- ◆ paint roller
- ◆ tape measure
- ◆ pencil
- ◆ masking tape
- ◆ blue, red, shocking pink and orange
- ◆ white glue or acrylic varnish

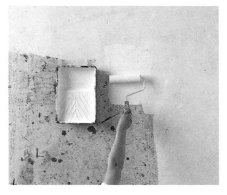

1 Give the floor two coats of white latex, to ensure that the colors of the design ring bright and true.

2 Measure and draw out your design. Tape off the border, which should have crisp edges. Do the same along the outside of the star.

3 Paint the star, then fill in the area inside the border; taping may not be necessary for this as a little white space between the star and border and background makes it look as though silk-screening has been used – a technique common in pop art. Seal the floor with diluted white glue or acrylic varnish.

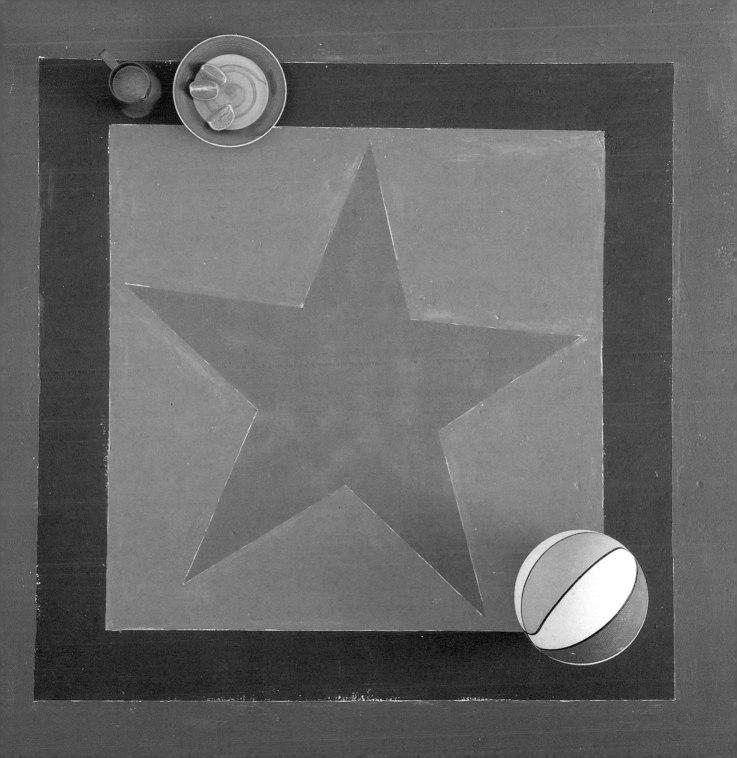

WOOD-GRAIN CHECKERBOARD

Checkerboards are a popular theme for flooring and yet are rarely seen in natural wood. If you are starting from a concrete or wooden floor, have the new floor covering cut into squares of the size you want and either screw them in place or stick them down. If your floor is already covered in sheets of plywood, fiberboard or hardboard, mark a checkerboard pattern, ignoring the natural seams. Woodgraining doesn't have to be done painstakingly carefully: you can alter the effect produced by the oil paint until it starts to dry. Obtain a sample for the wood effect; we used oak, grained to resemble wood treated in different ways, half "polished" and half "rough-sawn and sand-blasted." You could also use two different wood effects, such as walnut and maple.

YOU WILL NEED

- ◆ pencil
- ◆ tape measure
- ◆ long ruler or straightedge
- ◆ masking tape
- ◆ 2 cream oil-based eggshell paints
- ◆ paintbrushes
- ◆ wood sample
- ◆ artist's oil paints to match wood sample
- ◆ oil-based scumble or glaze
- ◆ paint thinner
- ◆ dry-graining brush
- ◆ graining comb
- ◆ satin varnish
- ◆ soft cloth
- ◆ non-slip polish (optional)

1 Make sure the surface is perfectly smooth, then mark off into checkerboard squares, if necessary. Edge alternate squares with strips of masking tape.

2 Using two different cream eggshell paints, paint alternate squares.

3 Mix the oil colors into the glaze, to match the wood sample. Thin with paint thinner, if necessary. For the "lighter" squares, brush on the glaze, in the direction you want the "grain" to appear to run, leaving the brush marks visible. ———————▶

4 Add random strokes.

7 Soften with a brush, adding paint thinner if the paint has dried.

10 Paint on more noticeable chevrons in the same way, following the grain.

5 After a few minutes, drag a dry-graining brush over to give the grain.

8 For the "darker" squares, repeat step 2.

11 Soften the effect, using the graining comb before the brush. Apply two coats of satin varnish and allow to dry. If you like, burnish with a little non-slip polish.

6 Using a darker oil paint and a fine artist's brush, gently draw in the chevrons of the wood grain.

9 Then repeat step 4, using a graining comb rather than a dry-graining brush, so the grain looks wider.

FIBERBOARD ROUTED

Black cork tiles over the whole floor in this room were too severe, but when the middle section of the room was treated to this wonderful soapstone effect, they became an important part of the overall grand gesture. The cork tiles in the center were replaced with a large piece of fiberboard, to which an intricate maze pattern was applied. This could simply have been painted onto plywood or fiberboard as a two-dimensional effect, but here the surface has been enhanced by routing the maze pattern (take it to a local joiner; routing really isn't for the inexperienced) and then painted to create a soapstone effect. You could also imitate slate, by using a wave formation and the black leading used for cleaning cast-iron fireplaces and grates.

YOU WILL NEED
- ◆ paper
- ◆ pencil
- ◆ fiberboard sheet
- ◆ plastic wood or wood filler, if necessary
- ◆ fine-grade sandpaper
- ◆ matte latex paint: white, dark gray and medium-gray
- ◆ paintbrushes
- ◆ candle
- ◆ scraper
- ◆ softening brush
- ◆ matte varnish

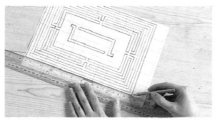

1 Plan your design on paper, using this picture as a guide. Draw it onto the sheet of fiberboard. Take it to a joiner to be routed and ask them to fix it in place on your floor. On an existing floor, draw the maze on the floor directly and ask a joiner to do the routing *in situ*.

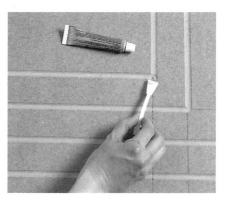

2 Fill any damage with plastic wood or wood filler, following the manufacturer's instructions. Don't try to achieve a perfectly flush surface at this stage. Allow to dry.

3 When dry, gently sand until you have a level surface. ⟶

4 Paint the whole surface white and allow it to dry.

5 Paint over the whole surface of the floor in dark gray.

6 Apply a generous coating of wax using a candle with circular movements.

7 Scrape off most of the candle wax, using a scraper.

8 Follow with a coat of medium gray.

9 Apply another coat of wax. Scrape off the wax, using a scraper.

10 Apply white paint with a dry softening brush to soften the whole effect. Seal with matte varnish. If you are surrounding the fiberboard with cork tiles, lay them at the end and butt them up to the edges neatly.

Opposite: Captivate your friends with this maze-patterned floor. The paint effect simulates soapstone but without the coldness or weight of that material.

CHECKED DOOR MATS

Floor mats are cheap and easy to come by, and you can often cut them without fraying the edges. They come in many finishes, some even incorporating words or pictures, and all in manageable rectangles.

When these very textured gray polypropylene mats are arranged with the pile running in different directions, a checkerboard effect is achieved. A combination of colors could be funky.

YOU WILL NEED
- ◆ string
- ◆ white crayon or chalk
- ◆ tape measure
- ◆ grey polypropylene door mats
- ◆ long metal ruler or straightedge
- ◆ craft knife
- ◆ notched spreader
- ◆ floor adhesive

1 Use strings to find the room's center (*see Techniques*) and mark with a cross. If possible, link the opposite pairs of walls. Measure the floor and work out how many floor mats you will need. Mark the cuts with a white crayon or chalk on the reverse of the floor mats.

2 If the mats are of carpet quality, score along the lines before cutting with the craft knife. Then cut the mats to size.

3 Using a notched spreader, apply floor adhesive to the floor.

4 Starting at the center, carefully lay the mats in position, remembering that, for the check effect shown here, you need to alternate the weaves.

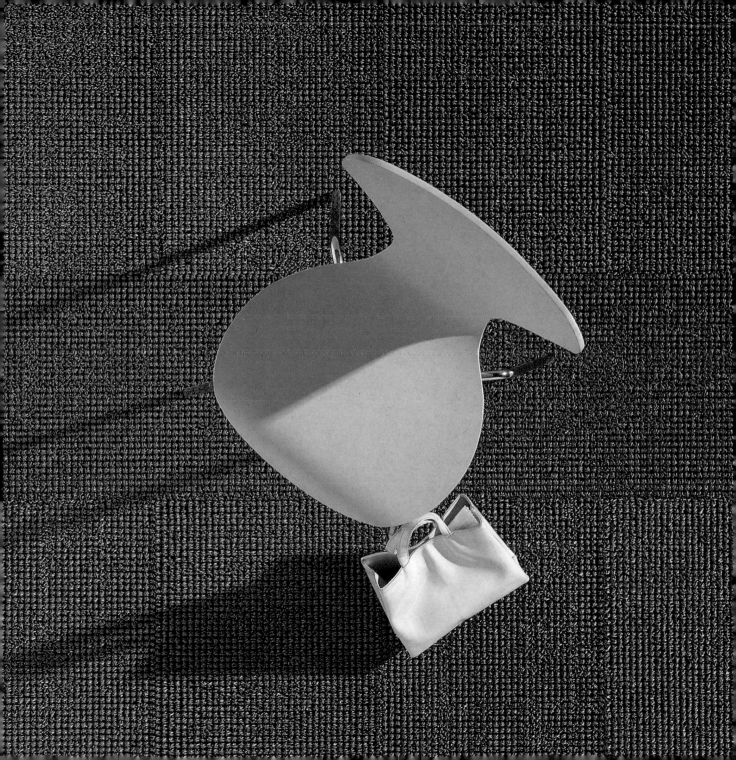

STENCILED HARDBOARD

Damaged or irregular floors are frequently covered in hardboard, and you may feel that this hard surface is in keeping if you have adopted a modernist, minimalist approach to decorating. In most cases, if you discover hardboard in mint condition, it is not wise to lift it, as it is probably hiding some horror below. However, with several coats of varnish, hardboard has a natural patina of its own, which is very appealing and works as a neutral background, as does a wooden floor. Introduce added interest by using stencils, which here mimic a fifties-style rug, though the brown hardboard would suit different colors. The contrast of black or white works well; choose a bold, non-figurative pattern.

YOU WILL NEED
- ◆ pencil
- ◆ paper
- ◆ black water-based paint
- ◆ paintbrushes
- ◆ metal ruler or straightedge
- ◆ masking tape
- ◆ cutting mat
- ◆ sheet of acetate
- ◆ craft knife
- ◆ pin
- ◆ stencil brush
- ◆ lint-free cloth or fine-grade sandpaper, if necessary
- ◆ eraser
- ◆ gloss varnish

1 Draw the border motif to the desired size on paper, using the template at the back of the book.

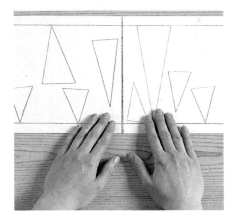

2 Photocopy the design and make sure that the pattern works by placing several sheets together.

3 Work out a right-angled section for the corners. Make sure it ties in neatly with the pattern on both sides.

4 Black in the design and photocopy it. Decide how far in from the edges of the room the border will be. Now lay the photocopies around the floor to ensure that your design will fit pleasingly, and experiment until you have an effect you are happy with.

5 With pencil, mark the outer edge of your border on the floor (in the photograph, this is about 5½in from the edge of the room).

6 Draw out pencil guidelines for your border all around the room.

7 Stick one of the photocopies to the cutting mat with masking tape. Tape the acetate over it.

8 Using the steel ruler and holding the knife at an angle, carefully cut out the stencil. To help get neat, sharp corners, make a pinprick just at the corner first; this also helps to prevent you from cutting too far.

9 With masking tape, attach the stencil to the hardboard, lining it up with your guidelines.

10 Using a stencil brush, stipple in the neat black triangles, making sure that the paint does not seep under the stencil.

11 Lift up the stencil and re-position it for the next section. Remember to make sure the underside of the stencil is clear of paint. If you need to mask certain areas of the stencil so that you continue the pattern when working the corners, do this with a piece of paper held in place with masking tape.

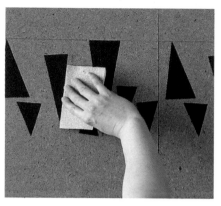

12 If you make a mistake or slightly smudge the stenciling, either quickly rub it clean with a damp cloth or, if the surface is more porous, very gently sand away the paint when dry. Finally, remove the pencil guidelines with an eraser and seal the floor with at least two coats of varnish, paying particular attention to the stenciled areas.

Right: Hardboard floors are practical but not usually glamorous; however, hardboard can gain its own natural patina with layers of varnish, and the addition of a bold, graphic stenciled border enhances the earthy and rugged feel of the floor to create a really strong impact.

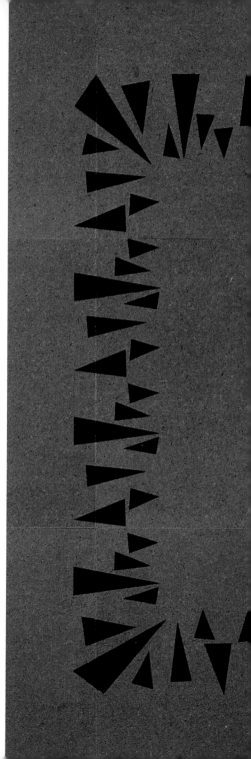

RUBBER MATS

Available from rubber manufacturers, this rubber safety matting is valued for its non-slip and protective qualities and, since it is waterproof, it is particularly useful in, say, a bathroom. It comes on a roller in a broad spectrum of colors, widths and textures. It doesn't fray and will absorb any lumps or strange seams in a floor. Clean and seal the matting with a silicone spray polish.

YOU WILL NEED

- ◆ 2 types of rubber safety mat
- ◆ tape measure
- ◆ metal rule or straightedge
- ◆ craft knife
- ◆ rubber tiles in different patterns
- ◆ rubber contact adhesive
- ◆ WD-40 or silicone spray

1 Measure the floor and the rubber matting, and carefully trim long runners to size.

2 For the corners, cut four squares. Divide these diagonally and make four squares by placing two triangles together, with the grooves running across top to bottom. Position these and the runners around the perimeter of the room.

3 Cut pieces from the other matting to fit the central section. Cut the tiles into squares, then cut holes in the mat to fit with the contrasting squares.

4 Secure all the pieces with rubber adhesive, applied to both surfaces. Spray with WD-40 or silicone spray.

DISTRESSED FLOORBOARDS

Wooden floors are often appealing because of their subtle variations of color that improve with age. Your wooden floors may not be in a great state to begin with, though, or may look uninteresting, and you don't really want to wait for the years to work their magic naturally. Wood stains can help to imitate that look in only a few hours. The look of driftwood or weathered teak or other hardwood decking, such as is found in beach houses, is the aim. Achieve the outdoor look using three different wood dyes and a wash of white latex, diluted almost to water. This technique would give a bleached effect to any wood stain; for example, over a warm mahogany, which would be otherwise quite dark, a wash of cream or white instantly gives the faded look of maturity.

YOU WILL NEED

- ◆ nail punch
- ◆ hammer
- ◆ power sander and fine-grade sandpaper
- ◆ wire brush
- ◆ 3 different wood stains of the same make
- ◆ lint-free cloth or paintbrushes
- ◆ rubber gloves
- ◆ white or cream latex paint
- ◆ dry cloth
- ◆ matte polyurethane floor varnish

1 It's important that floors have no sharp or protruding nails, so knock in any you find with a nail punch before you begin (*see Techniques*). Remove old paint spills using a sander. Remember to change the sandpaper frequently, or you will damage the rubber seal of the sander.

2 Brush the boards with a wire brush along the direction of the grain, with an occasional cross stroke to produce a distressed effect.

3 Experiment with the stains, mixing colors together – a little should go a long way. Use scrap wood to test the effect before you commit yourself.

4 With either a lint-free cloth or a brush, apply the stain. This will stain anything porous, so wear rubber gloves and old clothes.

5 Start by applying a generous quantity of stain, but rub most of the extra off. Don't stop till you've finished the floor or there will be a definite line; keep the joins between areas random, and avoid overlapping parallel bands of stain.

6 It's better to do one thin coat all over and then go back to apply more coats, perhaps working the stain into knots or grooves with a brush to produce an uneven, weathered look.

7 While this is still wet, brush on a wash of the diluted white or cream paint, about one part latex to four parts water.

8 Using a dry cloth, rub off extra paint or apply more until you have the effect you want.

9 Apply two coats of clear varnish, sanding very lightly between coats.

GLOSSY TONGUE-AND-GROOVE

Tongued-and-grooved boards look wonderful with a gleaming shine; they have to be one of the most dynamic uplifts you can bring to a room. Gloss paint or floor paint is wonderfully durable and easily renewed if it's ever damaged. Use this floor in a room with a large window, if you can, and watch the dramatic effect of the sun streaming in and highlighting the gloss. Gloss paint allows detail to show, so it was a natural choice for these brand-new tongued-and-grooved boards, but if you like the effect of the dramatic color but have an old, beaten-up floor, a matte finish would be more forgiving. To lay a new floor of this type, a perfectly smooth and level subfloor, such as hardboard, chipboard or marine-grade plywood, is vital (see Techniques for how to lay these).

YOU WILL NEED
- ◆ tongued-and-grooved boards
- ◆ hammer
- ◆ drill, with pilot drill bit
- ◆ flooring pins
- ◆ pin hammer
- ◆ nail punch
- ◆ power sander, with coarse-, medium- and fine-grade sandpaper
- ◆ undercoat paint
- ◆ paintbrushes
- ◆ high-gloss floor paint

1 Slot the tongued-and-grooved boards together and, using an offcut to protect the exposed tongue, tap the next board into place until it fits tightly. If the boards are warped, pin one end first and work along the board; in this way you will be able to straighten out the warp.

2 To prevent the tongues from splitting, pre-drill pilot holes.

3 Tap pins in gently, using a pin hammer, at a slight angle back toward the boards. →

4 Punch the pins in with a nail punch so the next board can butt up.

6 Lightly sand the whole floor again, to make it smoother. Finally, paint the whole floor with your chosen gloss paint.

5 When the floor is laid, and before finishing it, sand the floor, first with a coarse-grade sandpaper, and then with medium-grade and finally with fine-grade. Always sand in line with the wood grain. With long, even strokes in the direction of the grain, undercoat the floor. Allow to dry.

Right: Tongued-and-grooved boards are more often associated with wainscotting in country-style kitchens, but they make an easily laid flooring, too. A high-gloss, intensely colored finish is used here to stunning effect in a contemporary setting.

SHEET-METAL TREAD MATS

Sheet-metal tread plates are a very versatile flooring. They may be painted but look dazzling left in their natural state. Sheet-metal wholesalers offer a wide range of metals, such as copper, zinc and more, and will cut the sheets to size. They can be laid on concrete or on a subfloor of hardboard, chipboard or marine-plywood (see Techniques).

YOU WILL NEED
- ◆ wood scrap
- ◆ drill, with metal pilot drill bit, and wood drill bit, if necessary
- ◆ sheet-metal tread plates
- ◆ metal file
- ◆ wood screws, if necessary
- ◆ screwdriver
- ◆ floor adhesive, if necessary

1 Using a metal file, file away any rough edges, being careful not to create file marks on the visible top surface of the sheets.

2 Using a small piece of wood and a metal pilot drill bit, drill holes in every corner of the plates and at every 12in along the sides, depending on the size of the sheets.

3 If you're laying metal sheets on a wooden floor, screw through the holes in the metal into the wood surface with wood screws.

4 Butt up the sheets together and continue screwing them to the floor. If you have a concrete floor, these sheets can be glued directly in place. To finish, fit metal or wooden quadrant beading around the edges.

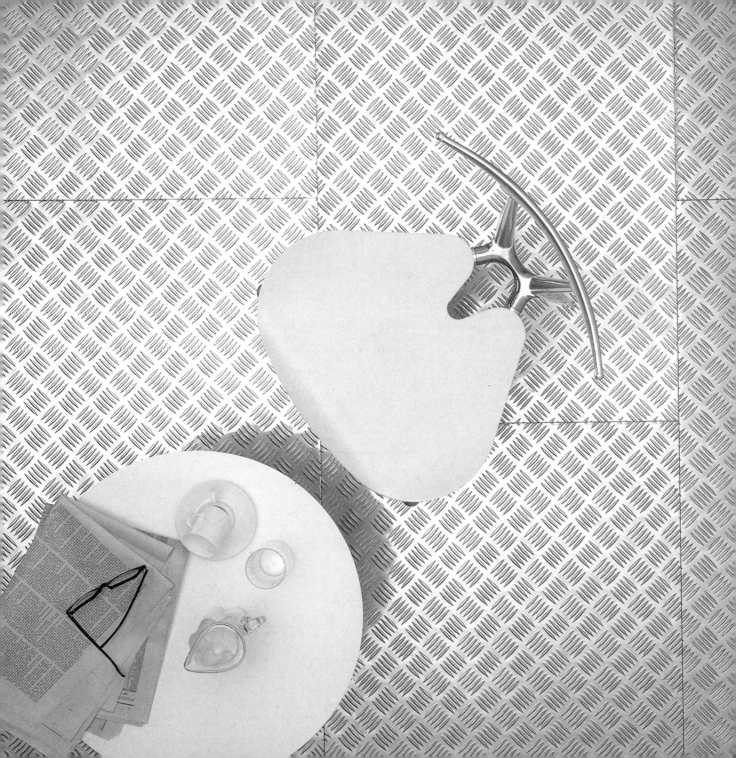

GOLD PAINT AND SCRIM FLOOR

In the past, only travelers to far-off countries could furnish their homes with exotic tables, fabrics, pots and statues, but today such ethnic treasures are widely available and sometimes require a more dramatic backdrop than subtle monotones.

Gold, copper and silver strike a note of flamboyance, but texture is also needed if the scheme is to be a rich foil for your possessions. Builders' scrim, used to reinforce plaster, fits the bill. It gives a wonderful surface that traps different amounts of gold and copper, creating the effect of beaten metal. It allows for a play of patterns such as tartans and checks that would otherwise be difficult to regulate. As with all exotic finishes, the delight here lies more in the instant transformation than in practicality.

YOU WILL NEED

- ◆ tape measure
- ◆ pencil
- ◆ paper and ruler
- ◆ power sander, with fine-grade sandpaper
- ◆ builders' scrim
- ◆ scissors
- ◆ wide paintbrush
- ◆ white glue
- ◆ oil-based gold paint
- ◆ copper powder paint
- ◆ heavy-duty floor varnish

1 Measure your floor. Taking into account the width of the scrim, plan your design on paper first, to make sure that your chosen tartan or check pattern doesn't leave you with an awkward half line at the edges of the room.

2 You need a smooth, flat surface to work on. If necessary, lay a marine-grade plywood or hardboard floor (*see Techniques*). Lightly sand the floor to make sure it's perfectly flat.

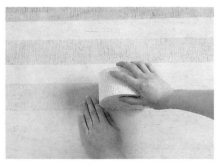

3 Cut the lengths of scrim, beginning with the longest, and lay it to your chosen pattern. Conceal seams at points where two lengths cross over, hiding the seam underneath, and over-lapping the ends by at least 6in. ⟶

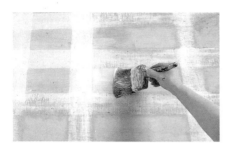

4 Stick the scrim down with white glue. Brush out any glue that soaks through to the top to hold the scrim firmly. Don't worry if you spread glue outside the area of the scrim. Pencil in a few guidelines and put a weight on the other end of the scrim to keep it straight.

6 Paint on the gold paint with the wide brush, covering the whole floor. If using an oil-based paint, make sure you have plenty of ventilation in the room. Allow to dry.

8 Apply at least two coats of heavy-duty floor varnish to seal.

5 Dilute the glue with water and coat the whole floor, going over the stuck-down scrim as well. This seals the floor and makes a good surface for the paint.

7 Dust the copper powder paint over the scrim, allowing it to be trapped by the mesh surface.

LINOLEUM IN 3-D PATTERNS

Linoleum now comes in many thicknesses, colors and patterns, and while it doesn't quite have the appeal of a beautiful classical floor, by cutting it into trompe l'oeil patterns and playing with slight color variations you can create grand effects. Aside from the fact that linoleum is hard wearing, water-resistant and probably one of the least expensive floor coverings, given this dramatic treatment, it can become the centerpiece of any hall, kitchen or bathroom that is free of furnishings most of the time. Rolls of linoleum and floor adhesive were used in this project but you could also use self-glued tiles to make a floor reminiscent of a Venetian palazzo. For this technique you need patience, exact templates and the kind of mind that adores jigsaw puzzles.

YOU WILL NEED

- ◆ power sander, with fine-grade sandpaper
- ◆ tape measure
- ◆ pencil
- ◆ paper
- ◆ ruler
- ◆ long metal ruler or straightedge
- ◆ linoleum rolls in different colors
- ◆ hardboard sheet
- ◆ saw
- ◆ craft knife
- ◆ contact floor adhesive

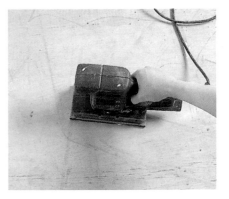

2 Having made sure no nail heads are exposed, lightly sand the floor, to make sure it's perfectly flat.

1 You need a smooth, flat surface on which to apply the linoleum. If necessary, lay a marine-grade plywood or hardwood floor (*see Techniques*).

3 Measure your floor. To ensure a good fit, it's very important to work out your pattern on paper first, using the template at the back of the book.

4 Draw grid lines on the floor as a guide when the laying the linoleum.

5 Using a piece of hardboard, draw each of the pattern shapes and cut them out carefully with a saw.

6 Use these templates to cut out the shapes. Remember that, unlike carpet tiles, linoleum isn't very forgiving and accuracy is all-important.

7 Try out your pattern in pieces of linoleum and see if any need trimming. If necessary, number them on the backs to help you fit them together.

8 Using contact adhesive, apply glue to the floor and the backs of the tiles and fit them in place; you cannot adjust them once they are laid.

Opposite: Reminiscent of Escher's unique drawings, this eye-deceiving, "three-dimensional" design is executed in shapes cut from linoleum. You are limited only by your own imagination in using this technique to produce individual masterpieces.

FAKE-FUR ANIMAL-SKIN RUG

A blown-up version of the baby on a sheep-skin rug theme, this idea is scaled up for a full-size rug. Rather than making a classical bear- or lion-skin rug, be more tongue-in-cheek, with shapes such as prehistoric dinosaurs or farm animals. Fake furs now come in bright colors, so you could take the concept even further from reality; mix up shapes and patterns.

YOU WILL NEED
- ◆ large sheet of tissue paper
- ◆ pencil
- ◆ long ruler
- ◆ dressmaker's pins
- ◆ fake fur fabric
- ◆ scissors
- ◆ thick felt
- ◆ pinking shears
- ◆ iron-on hemming strip and iron, or sewing machine, or sewing needle and matching thread

1 Draw a line down the middle of the paper, then draw half the bear shape on one side, following the template at the back of the book. Fold in half along the line and cut out the shape.

2 Enlarge the paper pattern to size, then pin it to your fur fabric

3 Cut your shape out and then cut the shape out again from the felt, using pinking shears. Include a 2½ in allowance all round.

4 Stick the wrong side of the fur shape to the right side of the felt shape with the hemming strip. Alternatively, either machine or hand sew the two fabrics together.

VERMEER-STYLE MARBLE

You may be faced with a hardboard floor and long for the grandeur and impact of a marble one. Marbling is relatively easy to do. A wonderfully strong pattern is used here, taken from Vermeer's Old Master paintings. You may choose to do a simple checkerboard or behave as if you had a huge slab of marble – which is wildly expensive when real. Find a small piece of marble as reference, as there is such a variety of marbles to choose from, and your floor's effect depends on understanding how the veins of your particular marble run. This technique of flooring is not suitable for anywhere where there is a lot of moisture, such as a bathroom, but a marbled dining room could look amazing.

YOU WILL NEED

- tape measure
- paper
- pencil
- ruler
- black felt-tipped pen
- white undercoat paint
- paint roller
- long straightedge, e.g. skirting length
- oil-based glaze
- artist's oil colors: light and dark gray, black and silver
- paintbrushes
- lint-free cloth
- bird's feather or quill
- softening brush
- dry cloth
- fine artist's brush
- black oil-based eggshell paint
- paint thinner
- matte varnish

1 Measure your room, then draw a scale plan and a grid on it, using the template at the back of the book.

2 Fill in your design, starting from the middle point of the floor and working out to the edges.

3 You need a very flat surface, such as hardboard or marine-grade plywood (*see Techniques*). Undercoat the floor with a couple of coats of white paint.

4 Draw the design on the floor in pencil. Put a blob of black paint in each square that is going to be painted black.

5 Add a little gray oil paint to the glaze and apply it very thinly, using a brush, to all the squares which don't have black dots and will therefore be white "marble."

6 Add more color to the glaze by dotting small amounts of oil paint directly onto your brush. Apply selectively to some areas.

7 With a lint-free cloth, soften the glaze while it is still wet.

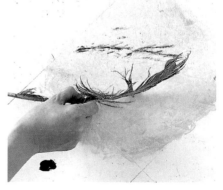

8 Take a bird's feather or quill, dipped into a mixture of black paint thinned with a little glaze, and gently draw across the surface, to simulate the veins. →

9 Use the softening brush to blur the outlines of the veining and blend them with the background. Wipe the brush regularly on a dry cloth to avoid any smudges.

11 Clean up the edges of the pencil squares with the corner of dry cloth.

13 Using a little gray or silver paint, applied directly onto a brush moistened with paint thinner, soften the black in swirling motions to make it look like slate. Finally, give the floor several coats of varnish.

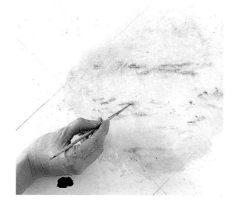

10 With a fine artist's brush, further soften the effect by adding paint thinner, which will blur the lines. You can also add more color or a second color, but remember to soften it again.

12 Carefully fill in the black squares indicated by the black dots.

Opposite: Marbling is one of the most dramatic paint effects, but it isn't too difficult to do if you take the stages slowly. If you have always dreamed of living in a palazzo *but actually reside in an apartment, create the cool, tranquil atmosphere of marbled-floor luxury for yourself.*

PATCHWORK CERAMIC TILES

Bathrooms, entryways and kitchens are often thought of as utility rooms, and their floorings are correspondingly spartan. But the wide range of ceramic tiles now available enables you to achieve stunning good looks without sacrificing practicality. Here we chose stylish blue tiles in the same color range accented by deep indigo.

YOU WILL NEED

- ◆ ceramic tiles
- ◆ pencil
- ◆ ruler
- ◆ tiling guide, if necessary
- ◆ tile adhesive (waterproof for bathrooms; flexible if on a suspended floor)
- ◆ notched spreader
- ◆ tile spacers
- ◆ squeegee
- ◆ grout
- ◆ damp sponge
- ◆ lint-free dry cloth
- ◆ dowel scrap

1 Draw a grid on the floor for the tiles (*see Techniques*).

2 Spread some adhesive on the floor. As you lay the tiles, use spacers to ensure even gaps between them. Use a straight-edge to check that all the tiles are horizontal and level. Use a squeegee to spread grout over the tiles and fill the seams.

3 Wipe off the extra grout with a damp sponge before it dries.

4 Buff with a dry cloth when the grout has hardened, then smooth the grout with the piece of dowel.

MATERIALS

As floors are often made of heavy-duty materials, some of the projects require special tools, such as a power sander and tile cutters. These can be rented from any good hardware shop.

Your basic tool kit should include an electric drill, screwdriver, tape measure, hammer, a long straightedge (preferably metal), sharp scissors, a craft knife and spare blades, pliers, masking tape, a range of different types of sandpaper and a range of paintbrushes.

There are many different adhesives available on the market for sticking down floor surfaces. Consult your local supplier about the surface you are planning to lay and what type of glue you should use. If you are working with a solvent-based glue, follow the safety instructions on the packaging and make sure the area you are working in is well-ventilated.

Varnishes are used to protect paintwork from wear and tear. Like paints, varnishes come in both oil and water-based varieties and matte, satin or gloss finishes. If you have used an oil-based paint on your floor, you must use

an oil-based varnish to cover it. Also, if you have used water-based paint then use a water-based varnish. You can use a plain or tinted varnish depending on the effect you wish to create. When applying the varnish always use a clean brush that has not been used for the paintwork.

At all times safety precautions should be followed. You should never cut toward yourself when using sharp cutting tools; protective clothing should be worn when working with solvent-based materials; great care should be taken when working with heavy machinery.

Right: Measuring tape (1); carpet tiles cut to shape (2); hammer (3); craft knife (4); mirror head screws (5); glue sticks to go in a glue gun (6); builders' scrim (7); wire brush (8); nail punch (9); stencil brush (10); panel pins (11); scraper (12); saw (13); floorboard nails (14); ceramic floor tiles (15); parquet flooring blocks (16); domes of silence (17).

TECHNIQUES

Nearly all the projects in this book must be done on a clean, flat surface such as hardboard, marine-grade plywood or sanded floorboards. Shown here are a few basic guidelines for floor-surface preparation. If you are in any doubt about your ability to carry out these instructions then ask a professional to assist you.

Securing loose floorboards

For suspended wooden floors (boards laid over floor joists), start by lifting the old floor covering and checking that all the boards are securely fixed to their joists, and that they are reasonably flat and level. Loose boards will creak annoyingly when walked on, and raised edges or pronounced warping may show as lines through the new floor covering.

Use either cut nails or large, oval-headed nails to secure loose boards. When driving them near pipe or cable runs, take care not to pierce them; it is best to drive the new nails as close to existing nail positions as possible, for safety's sake.

YOU WILL NEED
◆ nail punch
◆ hammer
◆ drill, with wood pilot drill bit
◆ wood screws
◆ screwdriver

1 Drive in any nails that have lifted due to warping or twisting on the floorboards and then recess their heads slightly, using a nail punch.

2 If nails won't hold the floorboards flat against the joist, drill pilot and clearance holes and use wood screws to secure the boards firmly in place.

86

Laying hardboard or marine-grade plywood

Covering existing boards with a hardboard or marine-plywood underlay is an alternative to floor sanding as a way of ensuring a smooth, flat surface, ideal for more decorative floor coverings or for embellishing in its own right. Lay the boards in rows, with joints staggered from row to row, and pin them down with hardboard pins, driven in at 6in intervals. Lay separate strips above where you know there are pipe runs.

If you're going to lay glazed ceramic or quarry tiles on a suspended wooden floor, put down exterior-grade plywood to support their weight.

YOU WILL NEED

◆ nail punch
◆ hammer
◆ hardboard pins
◆ tack hammer

1 If hardboard sheets are used as an underlay for a new floor covering, start by punching in any raised nail heads all over the floor with a nail punch.

2 Nail the hardboard sheets to the floorboards at 6in intervals along the edges and at 12in intervals across the face of the sheet.

Sanding floorboards

Where old floorboards are very uneven, or you plan to leave them exposed but they are badly stained and marked, hire a floor-sanding machine. This resembles a lawnmower, with a drum to which sheets of sandpaper are fitted. A bag at the rear collects the sawdust; however, always wear a face mask when sanding floors. Also rent a smaller disk or belt sander for finishing off the edges.

If necessary, drive any visible nail heads below the surface. Start sanding with coarse-grade paper at 45° to the direction of the floorboards; then use medium- and fine-grade paper in turn, with the machine running parallel to the boards. Use the disk or belt sander to tackle the perimeter of the room where the large sander can't reach.

YOU WILL NEED

◆ floor sander, with coarse-, medium- and fine-grade sandpaper
◆ smaller disk or belt sander
◆ scraper
◆ sandpaper and sanding block

1 Use a floor sander to smooth and strip old floorboards. Drape the electric cord over one shoulder and raise the drum before starting the machine.

2 Run the machine at 45° to the direction of the floorboards and with coarse-grade sandpaper fitted, first in one direction, and then at right angles to the original passes.

3 Switch to a medium-grade sandpaper and run the sander back and forth, parallel with the grain of the boards. Finish off with fine-grade sandpaper.

4 Use a smaller disk or belt sander to strip areas close to the baseboards and door thresholds where the larger drum sander can't reach.

5 Use a scraper to remove paint or varnish from inaccessible areas, such as around pipes. Then sand the stripped areas smooth by hand.

Laying chipboard
You can level and insulate a concrete floor by laying a floating floor of chipboard over it. This provides an ideal subfloor for many of the projects described in this book.

YOU WILL NEED
◆ heavy-duty polythene sheets
◆ sticky tape
◆ polystyrene insulation boards
◆ tongued-and-grooved flooring-grade chipboard panels

1 Lay the polythene sheets.

2 Tape the sheet to the walls. Butt-joint the boards all over the floor.

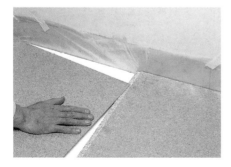

3 Cut the chipboard to fit and lay it over the insulation boards.

Setting out tiled floors

Like tiled walls, tiled floors need careful arranging if the end result is to look neat and professional. This is especially important with glazed ceramic and quarry tiles and also patterned vinyl and linoleum tiles; it matters less with plain vinyl and cork tiles, where the seams between the tiles are practically invisible.

Fortunately, the necessary setting-out is much easier with floor tiles than wall tiles, since you can dry-lay the tiles on the floor surface and move them around until you find a starting point that gives the best arrangement, with cut border tiles of approximately equal size around the perimeter of the room. In a regularly shaped room, start by finding the actual center of the floor by linking the midpoints of opposite pairs of walls with string lines. In an irregularly shaped room, place string lines so that they avoid obstructions, then link the midpoints of opposite pairs of strings, to find the room's center. Next dry-lay rows of tiles out toward the walls, in each direction, remembering to allow for the joint thickness, if appropriate, to

see how many whole tiles will fit in and to check whether this starting point results in over-narrow border tiles or awkward cuts against obstacles. Move the rows slightly to improve the fit if necessary, then chalk the string lines and snap them against the floor surface to mark the starting point.

YOU WILL NEED
- ◆ tape measure
- ◆ string and chalk powder
- ◆ drawing pins
- ◆ chalk

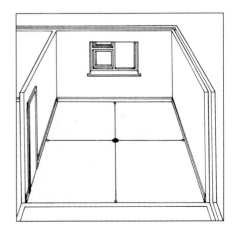

1 In a regularly shaped room, find the room's center by linking the midpoints of opposite walls with string lines. ⟶

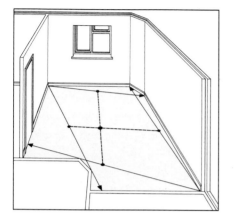

2 In an irregularly shaped room, use string lines that avoid obstacles, and link the midpoints of these, as shown, to find the center point.

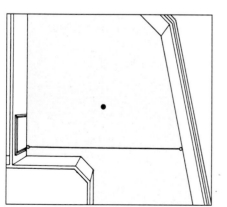

3 To ensure that tiles will be laid square to the door threshold, place a string line at right angles to it across the room to the opposite wall.

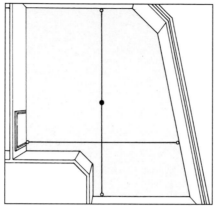

4 Place a second string line at right angles to the first, so that it passes through the room's center point.

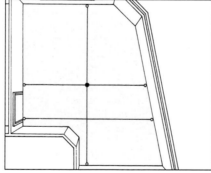

5 Place a third string line at right angles to the second, again passing though the center point, to complete the laying guide.

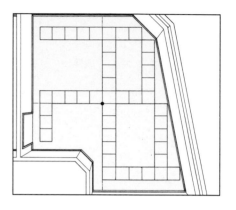

6 Dry-lay rows of tiles out from the center of the room toward the walls, allowing for the joint width between tiles as appropriate, to check the width of the border tiles and the fit around the obstacles.

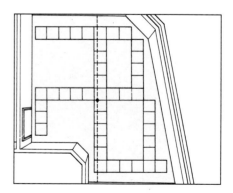

7 Adjust the string lines to get the best possible fit, chalk them and snap them against the floor to make the laying guidelines.

Laying ceramic floor tiles

Both glazed ceramic and quarry tiles can be laid directly over a concrete floor, as long as it is solid and dry. They can also be laid on a suspended timber floor, if it is strong enough to support the extra weight (check with a building surveyor). In this case, cover the floorboards with exterior-grade plywood, screwed down or secured with annular nails (ringed flooring nails) to prevent it from lifting; this will provide a stable, level base for the tiles.

Glazed ceramic floor tiles are laid with specially formulated adhesive, which should be waterproof in bathrooms and flexible if you're tiling on a suspended floor. Quarry and terra-cotta tiles are laid on mortar, over a solid concrete floor, and in thick-bed tile adhesive over plywood.

Lift old floor coverings before laying ceramic or quarry tiles, but if a solid floor is covered with well-bonded vinyl or cork tiles, leave these in place and tile over them, using tile adhesive. First, remove any wax polish on them.

Set out the floor as described on the previous spread, but transfer the starting point to the corner of the room farthest from the door, once the setting-out has been completed.

Remember to take off and shorten any room doors before laying floor tiles; and remove enough to allow the door to clear both the plywood underlay and the new tiles.

YOU WILL NEED
- ◆ pencil
- ◆ tiles
- ◆ lengths of wood
- ◆ pins
- ◆ tile adhesive
- ◆ notched spreader
- ◆ tile spacers
- ◆ large nail
- ◆ tile cutter
- ◆ squeegee
- ◆ grout
- ◆ damp sponge
- ◆ dowel scrap
- ◆ clean, dry, soft, lint-free cloth

1 Use a pencil and one of the tiles to mark up lengths of wood to use as a tiling guide. Allow for the width of the tile spacers. Pin tiling guides to the floor in the corner of the room, at right angles to each other, then spread some adhesive on the floor with a notched spreader.

2 Put the first tile in the angle between the tiling guides, butting it tightly against them and pressing it down firmly into the adhesive bed.

3 As the tiles are laid, use tile spacers to ensure an even gap between them. Use a straightedge to check that all the tiles are horizontal and level.

5 Cut the tile and fill the border gap. Continue to cut pieces from the offcut to fill the gap.

7 Use a piece of dowel or similar implement to smooth the grout lines, then buff the tiles with a clean cloth.

4 To cut border tiles, lay a whole tile over a tile laid against the tiling guide, butt another against the skirting board and mark its edge on the tile underneath with a nail.

6 Use a squeegee to spread grout over the tiles and fill all the joint lines. Wipe excess adhesive from the surface of the tiles with a damp sponge.

TEMPLATES

Photocopy montage

*Fake-fur animal
skin rug*

Linoleum 3-D in patterns

Stenciled hardboard

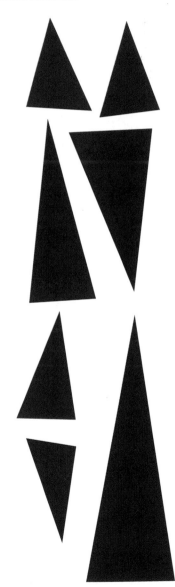

Vermeer-style marble

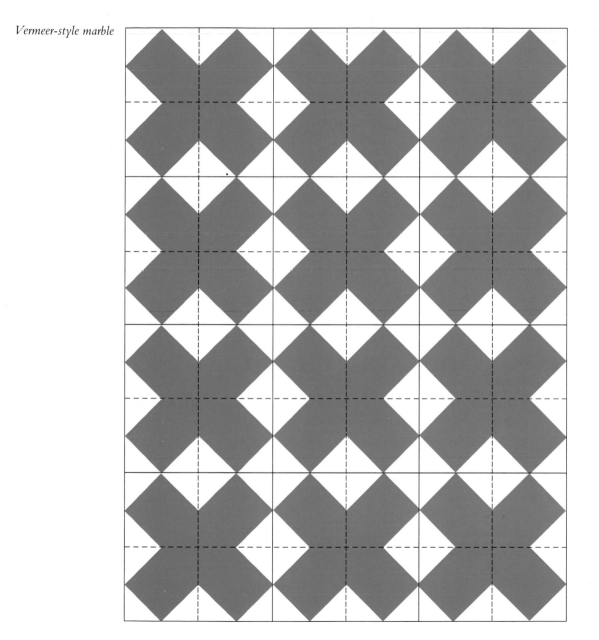

INDEX

Animal-skin rug, 76-7

Baseboards
    decorative, 14-15
    embellished, 16-17
Board game carpet tiles,
    25-7
Border, pistachio-shell, 22-4
Butterfly montage, 18-19

Carpet tiles, board game, 25-7
Ceramic floor tiles
    laying, 91-2
    patchwork effect, 82-3
Checked door mats, 54-5
Checkerboard, wood-grain,
    49-50
Chipboard, laying, 88-9
Color-washed parquet, 43-5

Decking, 36-7
Distressed floorboards, 62-4
Dry brush technique, 30-2
Duckboards, 36-7

Fake-fur animal skin rug, 76-7
Fiberboard routed floor, 51-3
Floating wooden flooring, 40-2

Floorboards
    sanding, 87
    securing loose, 86
    see also Wooden floors
Glossy paint, tongue-and-
    groove, 65-7
Gold paint and scrim floor,
    70-2

Hardboard
    laying, 87
    stenciled, 56-9
Herringbone pattern, color-
    washed parquet, 43-5

Japanese characters, 30-2

Linoleum in 3-D patterns,
    73-5

Marbling, Vermeer-style,
    78-81
Marine-grade plywood, laying,
    87
Materials, 84-5
Mats
    checked door mats, 54-5
    rubber mats, 60-1
    sheet-metal tread mats, 68-9
Metal tread mats, 68-9
Montages
    butterfly montage, 18-19
    photocopy montage, 33-5

Painted floors, 8-9
    distressed floorboards, 62-4
    fiberboard floor, 51- 3
gold paint and scrim floor,
    70-2
    glossy tongue-and-
        groove, 65-7

pastel stripes, 20-1
pop-art style floor, 46-7
stenciled hardboard, 56-9
Vermeer-style marble, 78-81
wood-grain checkerboard,
    49-50
Parquet, 38-9
    color-washed parquet,
        43-5
Pastel stripes, 20-1
Patchwork effect ceramic, 82-3
Photocopy montage, 33-5
Pistachio-shell border, 22-4
Plywood, laying, 87
Pop-art style floor, 46-7

Routed fiberboard floor, 51-3
Rubber mats, 60-1
Rugs, 10-11
    fake-fur animal-skin rug,
        76-7

Sanding floorboards, 87
Scrim, gold paint and scrim
    floor, 70-2
Sheet-metal tread mats, 68-9
Soapstone effect, fiberboard
    routed floor, 51-3
Stamps and dry brush, 30-2
Stenciling, 8
    stenciled hardboard, 56-9
Stripes, pastel, 20-1
Studded floor, 28-9

Techniques, 86-92
Templates, 93-5
Tiles, 12-13
    laying ceramic floor tiles,
        91-2
    patchwork effect ceramic,
        82-3

setting out, 89-90
Tongue-and-groove, glossy,
    65-7
Trompe l'oeil, linoleum in 3-D
    patterns, 73-5

Varnishing, 8-9
Vermeer-style marble, 78-81

Wood-grain checkerboard,
    49-50
Wooden floors
    color-washed parquet,
        43-5
    decking or duckboards,
        36-7
    distressed floorboards,
        63-4
    floating wooden flooring,
        40-2
    glossy tongue-and-groove,
        65-7
    parquet, 38-9
    techniques, 86-9
    wood-strip flooring, 40-2